Lamplight Collection of Modern Art

Picasso and the Cubists

Lamplight Publishing, Inc.
New York, New York

PUBLISHED IN THE UNITED STATES OF AMERICA IN 1975
by Lamplight Publishing, Inc., N.Y. 10016

First published in the series "Mensili d'Arte" Copyright c 1967
by Fratelli Fabbri Editori, Milan, Italy

Illustrations Copyright © 1970 by Fratelli Fabbri Editori, Milan,
Italy on the American Edition.

ALL RIGHTS RESERVED, PRINTED IN ITALY

Library of Congress Catalog Card Number: 70-1066-57
SBN 0-88308-010-9

The Birth of Cubism

In the early years of the twentieth century an art movement began which was not only to be the most productive and influential artistic development of its time, but which would also affect every phase of twentieth-century living in which design is a factor. A house, a chair, a necklace, a swimming pool, a theater, the textile for a drapery or a dress, all have been profoundly affected by the liberating force of the movement called "Cubism." All are different because of two men, Pablo Picasso and Georges Braque, and because of an art show that took place in Paris in 1908.

In that year Georges Braque submitted seven canvases to the Show of Independent Artists. Five were rejected and Braque withdrew all seven and exhibited them elsewhere. On the jury that rejected them was Henri Matisse, who described them rather scornfully as "entirely constructed of little cubes." Some time later a critic wrote in a Paris newspaper, "Monsieur Braque is an exceedingly daring young man. He has been emboldened by the puzzling experiments of Picasso...and unduly obsessed by Cézanne's style....He despises form and reduces everything, landscapes and figures and houses, to geometric patterns, to cubes." (The critic wisely added, "But we must not make fun of him. He is obviously sincere. Let us wait and see....")

And so the name Cubism was born. Actually it is a misleading and inaccurate name. Only in the first few years could it have been applied with any degree of aptness to the paintings it identifies. As a movement Cubism was so fertile, so adaptable, so readily expressive of the stylistic personalities of the various artists involved that it rapidly developed into new and different phases. After about 1911 or 1912 one no longer finds anything that might reasonably be described as a cube in Cubist painting. However, the Cubists accepted the name and exhibited under it.

Precursors: Post-Impressionism and Fauvism

Like other art movements, Cubism was the natural result of developments that preceded it, and at the same time it was the immediate creation of two individual artists, Picasso and Braque. Grandfathers of the movement were two great Post-Impressionists, Cézanne and Seurat. Great-uncles, since their influence, although important, was indirect, were two other great Post-Impressionists, van Gogh and Gauguin. A number of exhibitions shortly after 1900 focused the attention of the young artists in Paris on these older artists.

Inspired by the brilliant and expressive color of van Gogh and the flat color patterns of Gauguin, a number of painters formed themselves into a group called the "Fauves," or "Wild Beasts," headed by Henri Matisse. Braque was briefly a member of this group. Fauvism was a movement of rebellion against the rigid realism of academic art, a rebellion that would be carried much further by Cubism, which followed close on its heels and which, in many ways, opposed it. The two movements, continuing in a more violent way a rebellion begun thirty years earlier by the Impressionists, shared a common aim of artistic freedom but set about the achievement of it in very different ways. In fact there came to be a kind of rivalry between them, each studiously avoiding the characteristics that distinguished the other.

Seurat was of interest to the budding Cubists because of his scientific studies of color. But the greatest single impetus toward Cubism was provided by Cézanne with his feeling for the "architecture" that underlies nature, and with his statement that "everything in nature is based on the sphere, cone, and cylinder. One must first learn to paint according to these simple shapes...."

The derivation from Cézanne is so clearly visible in the paintings of the early years of Cubism that this phase in its development is often referred to as "Cézannesque Cubism." Not only are his forms imitated but his color too, even his brush stroke.

The first to follow, in landscape, Cézanne's reduction of natural forms to geometric shapes was Braque. He also appropriated Cézanne's limited palette of ochres, siennas, and blue-greens and his short, diagonal brush stroke, which was used to construct forms rather than simply to color them. An example is *Houses at L'Estaque* (Plate 4). "Line and color are inseparable," Cézanne had said. "In the act of painting, you are drawing." The early Cézannesque landscapes of Raoul Dufy, also painted at l'Estaque, are very similar (Plates 5 and 8).

In artists of lesser stature this influence shows as a mere mannerism, a kind of new and modern style in which they continued to paint representational pictures. But for Picasso and Braque, and such of their followers as truly understood the problem they were trying to solve, this Cézannesque phase was not a mannerism but the first step in a long process away from representational art and imitation of nature toward abstract art.

Picasso

The development of Cubism through its many phases—Analytical Cubism, Facet Cubism, Synthetic Cubism, Curvilinear Cubism, etc.—is marked by corresponding changes in Picasso's style. In fact the number of his stylistic changes make Picasso unique in the entire history of art. No other artist had ever painted in this way. In general an artist's style changes as his character unfolds and his powers ripen. He grows as a tree grows, from groping stem and tentative bud to full-blown flower and ripe fruit, straightforwardly and all-of-a-piece, quite consistently an oak or a linden or a sycamore. But Picasso is such a tree as never grew before. Each branch of him is different from every other branch, each produces a different exotic flower or fruit, and yet these varied branches are not grafted but grow marvelously and naturally from the same trunk.

And the frequency of Picasso's changes of style is matched by their drastic quality. Each is abruptly and violently different from the preceding one. "I have a horror of copying myself," Picasso says.

Born Pablo Ruiz, Picasso chose his mother's surname as being more distinctive. His own precocity plus his father's training—José Ruiz was an artist and teacher of art—brought him to a high level of technical ability at a very early age. At fifteen he was a completely trained artist, in an academic-realist way. Proof of his extraordinary achievement was the fact that he passed, in a single day, an examination at the School of Fine Arts in Barcelona which was so difficult that it generally required a whole month for its completion. He repeated this feat when he was awarded a scholarship to the Fine Arts Academy at Madrid. And at sixteen he had his first exhibit.

In 1900 he went to Paris for the first time. His first visits were tentative and exploratory, but in 1904 he settled there permanently in a ramshackle tenement-studio in Montmartre called the "Bateau-lavoir" (the floating laundry). He worked without models, sleeping during the day and painting at night.

His first Paris show in 1901 was not a success. Critics found in him no originality, only undigested borrowings from other artists, especially Toulouse-Lautrec. But Picasso was only twenty years old, and youthful exuberance may have interfered with his artistic digestion. Actually he was always a borrower, as he himself readily admits, but not an imitator. "I don't hesitate," he said, "if anyone shows me, for example, a collection of old drawings, to take from them anything I like." He has been called a "master thief." But what he takes he assimilates completely. It enters his bloodstream and becomes pure Picasso.

Picasso's early style, that of his Blue and Pink periods, was poetic but still quite realistic. He became suddenly dissatisfied with it as "all sentiment" and abandoned it, never to return to it again. It was at this point that he set out on his path away from realism and "literary" art. He had reached his technical maturity. The year was 1906 and he was twenty-five years old.

Two new influences now become apparent in his work. The first, which began during a summer spent at the village of Gosol in the Spanish Pyrenees, was that of primitive, pre-Roman, Iberian sculpture. A second influence was that of primitive Negro sculpture, which had come, quite by chance, to the attention of the Parisian art world. In 1900 Maurice Vlaminck noticed in a curio shop an intriguing little African figure carved in wood, and bought it. He placed it in Derain's studio, where Matisse noticed it and was so impressed by it that he began to collect other similar African statuettes and masks. His enthusiasm brought African sculpture to Picasso's notice. Whereas Matisse and the other Fauves had been interested in it primarily because of its primitive quality, which was in tune with their own fight against the too civilized realist art of the academies, Picasso appreciated it for its own esthetic value. He was fascinated by its simplified forms, its distortions for religious or expressive purposes, by the tremendous vitality that infused it, but most of all by its perfection as abstract design. He recognized that it was a beautiful arrangement of forms, quite apart from any ritual purpose or significance that it may have had.

Les Demoiselles d'Avignon (Plate 1) has been called the first Cubist painting. Whether it is or not may be a matter of debate, but in any case it marks Picasso's first really violent stylistic change. He left behind the sentimental melancholy of his Blue and Rose periods and embarked on something new.

He began the sketches for the painting in 1907. His early sketches are more descriptive, as in his previous manner, and show five female figures, one holding a skull, and two male figures, possibly sailors, but in the final painting the latter have been eliminated and the former reduced to abstract human shapes of rather indeterminate sex. Of this process of elimination, of paring away nonessentials so as to free the basic forms, Picasso has stated very succinctly, "In my case a picture is a sum of destructions."

In spite of the fact that he has, with *Les Demoiselles d'Avignon*, moved farther toward abstraction than Cézanne ever did, his derivation from the old master is clearly to be seen. Like Cézanne's *Grandes Baigneuses*, Picasso's painting is an architectural arrangement of nude female forms within a rectangular frame, the whole kept relatively flat. But it is the general spirit of the painting, more than any single quality, that relates it to Cézanne.

The two influences deriving from primitive sculpture, Iberian and Negro, show very clearly here. They show with such separate distinctness, in fact, that they disrupt the unity of the picture in a way that is disturbing. The faces of the three figures to the left, with their simplified forms and large, staring eyes, show the archaic Iberian derivation. The two figures to the right, startlingly unrelated to the others, show the African influence. This markedly different style is distinguished by its angularity of planes, by the masklike quality of the faces, distortion of features, and by the repeated parallel lines, which imitate the grooved texture of the original sculpture.

The dissonance between the two sets of figures is due to the fact that Picasso made his discovery of primitive African sculpture when he was midway through the painting. He had done the first three figures under the influence of Iberian sculpture, and then, in the flush of enthusiasm for his more recent discovery, he had changed styles while in the process of painting the picture and continued it under the African influence.

The colors are an equilibrium of warm rose and sienna and cool blues. Behind the figure to the extreme left is what appears to be a curtain. The remaining blue areas with their jagged planes seem to indicate a space that is as solid as ice or glass, more solid, perhaps, than the figures themselves.

The title of the painting was not Picasso's and was not attached to it until twelve years later. At that time a friend named it in joking reference to a brothel in Barcelona, although the brothel connotation is much more evident in the sketches than in the finished painting.

A few years earlier Picasso had met Gertrude Stein and her brother Leo. The Steins had become patrons as well as friends and he had done a portrait of Gertrude. Like his later *Demoiselles d'Avignon* this portrait marked a change in style. He had begun it in the manner of his Rose period, but after his summer at Gosol in the Pyrenees he had completely repainted it in the masklike manner of his (then) new Iberian style. Gertrude Stein made some remark about the quality of harshness, almost ugliness, that is frequently to be found in his painting and that seems to be somehow connected with his urgent creativity. It is generally an asset rather than a detriment and contributes to an effect of intense vitality. Miss Stein, in her best rose-is-a-rose fashion, quotes Picasso's reply to her observation: "When you make a thing, it is so complicated making it that it is bound to be ugly, but those that do it after you, don't have to worry about making it and they can make it pretty, and so everybody can like it when the others make it."

Analytical Cubism

The Cubist movement stems directly from the *Demoiselles.* Analytical Cubism begins here, the breaking down or "analysis" of natural forms into new, arbitrary forms and colors. The artist is not interested in creating an imitation or illusion of reality, but a new kind of reality, by means of a new artistic "language" of forms. Actually the *Demoiselles* is still comparatively realistic, but the representational element is no longer important and it becomes less and less evident as Cubism progresses, until it almost disappears.

André Derain

The Cézannesque phase persisted for a few years, both in Picasso's painting and in that of his followers. *Still Life on a Table* (Plate 12) by André Derain might almost have been painted by Cézanne himself, except that the distortions are more extreme in Derain's work. Cézanne's reverse perspective, his way of tilting up a table top to bring the more distant edge forward and thus reduce the depth of the picture, is here carried further by Derain. The discrepancy in viewpoint between the flat bases of the pitchers and their more rounded tops, and between the legs of the table and its top, is more violent. But in general tone the younger artist is the obvious disciple of the older.

Derain had been a Fauve before moving temporarily into Picasso's camp. His *Martigues* (Plate 7) makes use of the brilliant color of the Fauves in flat patterns that derive from Gauguin, and at the same time it shows a kinship with Cézanne's landscapes.

In 1908 Picasso experimented with Cubism in several different styles. *Dryad* (Plate 3) is a simplification of a nude female form rather like those in *Demoiselles.* *Woman with a Fan* (Plate 2) is closer in feeling to the abstractions that he would do in later years. The forms are simpler and very much flattened. The use of curves is limited, and preference is given to angular shapes and lines that relate to the rectangular shape of the picture. A year later in *Woman with Mandolin* (Plate 10) Picasso is experimenting with the blocklike and cylindrical and spherical forms that Cézanne had advised artists to find in nature.

Facet Cubism

But another more drastic stylistic change was about to make its appearance. This was Facet Cubism, in which the breakup of forms becomes almost explosive. Forms have been splintered into a multiplicity of tiny planes and then reassembled. The resulting shapes are crystalline, jewel-like. The trend toward simplification is completely reversed and the paintings become more and more complicated.

Facet Cubism explores a quality of Cézanne's painting that he had produced as a kind of by-product, without intending it and perhapes without even being aware of it. For lack of a word that describes it better, we call it "music," but it is a music that the eye enjoys rather than the ear. It is the interplay in a painting of planes and lines and angles, of brush strokes and colors and delicate tonal harmonies. To see this visual music one must close one's mind to any suggestion of reality in the painting, perhaps by turning it upside down or on its side, because the representational quality somehow distracts from that of the music. Braque and Picasso create this music intentionally, as a major effect in an art that is abstract, rather than as an accidental effect in representational art, as Cézanne had done.

A critical article on Matisse from the London *Times* applies quite as aptly to Picasso and Braque in this musical phase of Facet Cubism: "Most people look for beauty in a picture only in the objects represented, which they expect to remind them of beautiful real things. They have no notion of beauty created, not imitated, in a work of art, and created by the effort of expression. One may say, if one likes, that the artist is attempting things impossible to his art, that he is trying to turn painting into music. But one need not therefore fall into a rage and accuse him of incompetence or wilful perversity."

But Facet Cubism is still representational. The original subject is easily recognizable, as in *Seated Woman* (Plate 16) and *Violin and Palette* (Plate 17). In *Portrait of Ambroise Vollard* (Plate 18) the subject is not only recognizable but is an admirable likeness of the shrewd old art dealer.

A year later, however, the resemblance to reality had almost disappeared. In *Accordionist* (Plate 19) our only clue to the original subject of the painting is the title and the little set of keys, or valves, in the center of the picture. In *The Poet* (Plate 20) we have even less of a clue: the hint of a mustache amid shapes that are vaguely suggestive of delicate features.

It is noticeable that during this period of Cubism abstractions are built of straight lines rather than curves, with only an occasional small circle or arc as a kind of punctuation. Noticeable too is the very restricted palette. The paintings of this period are done in soft harmonies of brown, cream, and gray, sparked with black and white. Both of these restrictions are due partly to the influence of Cézanne and partly to the rivalry already mentioned between the Fauves and the Cubists. The Fauves expressed their artistic beliefs with bright, intense colors and curved lines, with emphasis more on decoration than expression or construction. And their work often has an almost childlike gaiety. By contrast, the Cubists' works are more formal and austere, and are structural rather than decorative. But the self-imposed restrictions of the Cubists, while resulting in exquisitely subtle harmonies of color and line, hindered the development of Cubism.

Georges Braque

From the beginning of Cubism its co-inventor, Georges Braque, had been matching Picasso picture for picture. In fact it was Braque who first broke up landscape forms in the manner of Cézanne, creating the paintings that gave Cubism its name. Frequently the two artists' work is very much alike, as they quite understandably influenced each other. But their personalities are very different and, except in certain phases of Cubism, their paintings are readily distinguishable. Picasso is far more violent, daring, and emotional: his temperament has a generous touch of Spanish fire. Braque is coolly reasonable, more aloof and reflective, not without emotion, but holding it in check. "Nobility," he says, "grows out of contained emotion."

The contrast in physical appearance of the two artists is as marked as that of their temperaments. Picasso was, according to the description of one of his friends, "small, swarthy, thick-set, restless and disquieting, with dark eyes that were strange, deep, piercing, almost fixed. Poorly and carelessly dressed, with the hands of a workman and awkward gestures...he looked half Bohemian, half laborer...." Braque, by contrast, was tall and well built, handsome, quiet-mannered, meticulous, private. His orderliness and logic provided a counter-balance to Picasso's brilliance and audacity.

Braque had originally been a Fauve, but he found himself out of tune with it. It was too flamboyant and disorganized for such an orderly temperament as his. "You can't remain forever in a state of paroxysm," he said.

In 1907 he met Picasso for the first time. A friend took him to Picasso's studio to see *Demoiselles,* which at first startled and dismayed him as it had all the other artists and friends who had seen it. Matisse thought it was some kind of hoax to discredit art, and Braque exclaimed that Picasso was serving up "cotton rags washed down with turpentine."

But in spite of his bewilderment he sensed that Picasso's painting objective was akin to his own. Indeed, in 1908 and 1909 the two artists followed parallel paths and explored the same problems before joining forces in the autumn of 1909 in what was to be one of the most remarkable partnerships in the history of art. "We were like two climbers roped together on a mountain," Braque said.

In total output, and certainly in the almost measureless impact of his influence, Picasso far outstripped his friend and fellow artist. But if one compares individual paintings of the two artists, Braque is often Picasso's equal and occasionally his superior. His work is smoother, more tasteful and harmonious, with a special kind of elegance that is peculiarly his own. And it is almost invariably beautiful. Picasso's work is rougher, frequently unbalanced, more powerful, more vital, more intense, and often less beautiful.

While not as restlessly creative as Picasso, Braque is nevertheless to be credited with some of Cubism's most startling innovations. He was the son of a house painter and decorator, and consequently had always been acquainted with such decorator's paraphernalia as sample books of wallpaper, wood veneer, marbling, and lettering. He was also acquainted with the techniques for imitating decorative effects, such as the use of a comb to obtain the effect of wood grain. It was Braque who first began to incorporate these elements into his paintings, at first by imitating them and then by making use of the actual material. In *Valse* (Plate 21) he imitates wood graining for textural and decorative effect.

When lettering is introduced into a painting, as it is here, it is often for decorative purposes only, not because of the significance of the words. In this case, however, there are obvious musical implications throughout the picture that are pointed up by the printed word "valse": the curves that suggest the shapes of violins and cellos, the central form resembling a fiddle neck, wood graining like that of a stringed instrument, circular holes like those in a violin's sound box, and in the upper left part of the picture a pair of tuning keys. Conversely, in *Still Life on a Table* (Plate 26), the letters used have no other purpose in the painting than a decorative one.

Lettering is used in still another way by Picasso in *The Aficionado* (Plate 27). Here it provides a clue to the subject of a painting that might otherwise be too obscure for the observer. It is a key for deciphering a sometimes baffling language. "TOR" and "Torero" set the theme as having to do with bullfighting, and "Nimes," the site of a large and well-known bullring, reinforces it.

On the general subject of the use of lettering in art one critic wrote, "Picasso and Braque incorporated in some of their pictures letters from labels and other printed matter, because label, notice and advertisement play a very important role in the modern city, and are well-suited for incorporation into works of art."

Braque was also the first to use "fool the eye" technique in his work, painting some small object into his abstraction so realistically that the viewer is tempted to touch it. In *Violin and Palette* (Plate 17) he has painted just such a realistic nail, with its cast shadow, at the top of the painting. This nail results in two interesting effects. It reverses the traditional composition of a still life, which is from a base, such as a table, upward, and makes the entire arrangement appear to hang suspended. And its incongruous realism in the midst of the other fragmented and unrealistic forms puzzles the observer and disturbs him with its small mystery, which is exactly what Braque intended it to do.

Collages

From these innovations it was only a short step to the actual incorporation of a real object into the picture, as the oilcloth in Picasso's *Still Life with Chair Caning* (Plate 25). The materials most frequently used were bits of wallpaper or newspaper, postage stamps, matchboxes, or rope. Braque, for textural effect, sometimes mixed sand with his paint.

These "collages" struck still another blow at the traditional idea of what a painting should be. The notion that these ordinary materials, usually considered inferior and inartistic, could be made meaningful in a work of art, was a revolutionary one. And it also posed the question to the observer as to which was more real, the physical object incorporated into the painting or the painting itself.

Synthetic Cubism

At this stage in the development of Cubism the possibilities of "analysis" had been carried as far as they could go and a reaction had begun that came to be called Synthetic Cubism. Whereas Analytical Cubism had begun with a real object and broken it down, Synthetic Cubism takes a real object as a kind of theme or idea on which to improvise and construct. The welter of faceted forms is done away with. The planes are larger and simpler and the designs are stronger. Textures are more varied and interesting.

An example of Synthetic Cubism is *The Violin* (Plate 28). Here Picasso has taken the violin as a motif and has woven around it a composition that is interesting and beautiful on its own account. It is neither descriptive of a violin, as a representational painting would be, nor is it an "analysis" or breakup of a violin form, as earlier Cubist treatment would have made it. Instead it evokes and suggests its subject.

The words "Jolie Eva" which appear here have, as far as the actual painting is concerned, only a decorative purpose. But they mark an event in Picasso's life, his new love for Marcelle Humbert, who superseded Fernande Olivier in his affections. He called her "Eva" and incorporated her name into his paintings at that time, rather the way a young boy carves his initials with those of his sweetheart in the bark of a tree.

Musical motifs occur so frequently in the work of both Picasso and Braque that there may be some connection, intentional or otherwise, between them and the "visual music" of abstraction that was mentioned earlier. Musical connotations are present in Braque's *The Musician's Table* (Plate 30) in the curving violin or guitar shapes, circular sound-box holes, fine parallel lines like sheet music, and in the introduction into the center of the composition of the first three letters of the word "valse."

After World War I the abstractions of Picasso and Braque become richer and more varied in color, and are constructed of curved rather than angular shapes. Braque's still lifes of the twenties (Plates 34 and 35) are masterful decorative achievements. In design they are flawless, in color luxurious. Their quality of distinctive elegance is a stamp of his personality quite as unmistakable as his signature. One still feels his sense of measure, of restraint, his belief that progress in art "does not consist in extending its limits, but in knowing them better."

Juan Gris

During these years other talents than those of Picasso and Braque were finding expression in Cubism. One of the most able of these was that of Juan Gris, who was perhaps the only other Cubist whom Picasso and Braque found interesting. His aim in his painting was, as he put it, "to create new combinations of known elements." Like the others, he was influenced by Cézanne, but he said, "Cézanne goes toward architecture. I start out from it."

Gris had moved into a studio in the delapidated "floating laundry" just as Picasso was beginning work on *Les Demoiselles d'Avignon.* Thus he was present at the very beginning of Cubism. But in spite of the fact that he learned a great deal from Picasso, he was never an imitator. He followed his own bent. Cubism, sifted through his personality, produced art that was very different from Picasso's and Braque's although based on the same premises.

His *Portrait of Picasso* (Plate 22) is not, like the latter's painting of Ambroise Vollard (Plate 18), a portrait as well as an abstraction. It bears no resemblance whatsoever to Picasso. What interests Gris is the play of light across planes and facets and sharp-edged contours. His method was like that of Picasso, as the latter once explained it: "When I paint a picture I am not concerned with the fact that two people may be represented in it. Those people once existed for me, but they exist no longer. My vision of them gave me an initial emotion, then little by little their presence became thinned....Then they disappeared altogether, or rather they became for me no longer people, but forms and colors."

The earliest Cubist paintings of Gris are done with a limited palette, but not the same limited palette as Picasso's and Braque's. Gris preferred shades of gray and gray-blue to their brown shades. He has been called "the most Cubist of the Cubists"—perhaps in slightly humorous reference to the fact that his paintings actually contain suggestions of cubes. *Gray Still Life* (Plate 23) is an exquisitely ordered arrangement of forms that are obviously derived from real objects, painted in the most delicate and harmonious colors. With the Cubist multiple viewpoint we see the water glass simultaneously from above and from the side, and the table and fruit dish in the same way except that the two views, profile and top, are treated as separate forms.

The later collage *Still Life with Fruit Dish and Carafe* (Plate 31) uses the same elements that Picasso and Braque used, for the same purposes, but in a completely different style. Fragments of newspaper, wallpaper, and marbling are used both decoratively and as a means of fixing the positions of the various planes in a space that is shallow but not entirely flat. The bit of newspaper, for instance, appears to float on top of all the other planes and marks the outermost point of the space that Gris has created. The deepest space is the area of black. Intermediate planes waver, because of the transparency of the objects drawn over them, in a way that is puzzling and pleasing. The irregular shape of pink marbling is behind the water bottle, and yet its bottom edge protrudes over the plate, which is obviously in front of it. The transparent plate is cut through with a solid fragment of itself viewed from the back. The rectangle underneath the piece of newspaper is both under and on top of the striped cloth.

Gris soon abandoned his restricted palette. The colors in *Three Cards* (Plate 33) are wonderfully rich and satisfying and their relationships quite extraordinarily beautiful. And the arrangement of forms is as pleasing as the color: the relation, for instance, of the three small circles to the larger circular planes of the table top, and the interjection of the sharp, angular planes between them, dividing and yet uniting them. Many critics consider this painting one of the finest achievements of the Cubist movement.

Fernand Léger

Another important and totally different personality was that of Fernand Léger. He based his style on forms that were more contemporary than those of the other Cubists. His inspiration was the newly mechanized world around him, and the forms he chose to use were those of the machine.

Of his *Nude Figures in a Wood* (Plate 37) he wrote: "I had an obsession. I was set on 'disjointing' bodies. You know what they called me — a 'Tubist'! I spent two whole years tussling with volume in *Nude Figures in a Wood....* It was solely a battle of volumes."

A little later Léger began to experiment with "contrasts of forms." In *Woman in Blue* (Plate 38) he set large, flat shapes against the smaller tube-like forms that are characteristic of him. As Picasso and Braque frequently did, he introduced fragments of realistically painted objects into a composition that was basically abstract. In the right center section of the painting is a corner of a table, drawn in conventional perspective, and the decorated profile of a vase. No matter how far Cubism may wander into abstraction, it never completely severs itself from the world of reality.

Léger is reported to have said that the sight of a gleaming cannon barrel during World War I revolutionized his conception of painting. This may account for the change in style that is to be seen in *Woman in Red and Green* (Plate 40) and *Soldier with Pipe* (Plate 43) although his predilection for cylindrical forms was apparent much earlier.

Léger was one of the artists who exhibited in the famous Room 41 at the Show of Independents in 1911. Picasso and Braque steadily refused to exhibit except at their dealers' galleries, and so it was left to other Cubists to bring the movement to the attention of the public. With Léger as exhibitors in Room 41 were Jean Metzinger, Albert Gleizes, Henri Le Fauconnier and Robert Delaunay.

Robert Delaunay

The public received the new art with its customary indignation and the critics with their customary hostility. Particular targets for their displeasure were two paintings by Robert Delaunay, *The Eiffel Tower* (Plate 54) and *The City* (Plate 55). The former was described by one critic as "an Eiffel Tower toppled over, presumably with an eye to destroying the nearby houses which, dancing a cancan, are rudely sticking their chimney pots into each other's windows."

Actually, Delaunay was one of the most original and creative of the new Cubists. His particular interest was in the effects of light. He observed the changes that light can make in the shapes of objects, especially buildings, bending and breaking outlines and planes, or disintegrating them entirely. These broken lines and twisted forms led to the term "catastrophic art" for such works of his as *Eiffel Tower* and *The City*. He apparently accepted it as a descriptive rather than a derogatory term, because he himself later referred to this phase of his art as his "Destructive period."

A number of lesser but still authentic artists played variations on the Cubist theme. They were apart from the central, creative, pioneering thrust of Cubism and adapted and experimented with it. But since one of the strengths of Cubism was its capacity for variation and development, these contributions added to its scope and importance.

Jacques Villon

Jacques Villon (his real name was Gaston Duchamp) came under Cubism's influence second hand, through his artist brothers Marcel and Raymond. Traces of it are to be seen in his portrait of Raymond (Plate 52), but he adapted it in a more personal way later on. In *Soldiers on the March* (Plate 42) his subject is not the soldiers, but their movement. Rhythmic line is seen as his first interest, while color is only secondary, an additive rather than an integral part of the structure. "The line of the vital urge in all things," Villon called the rhythm that he was trying to express.

While Villon was not a Futurist, his interest in movement relates him to them. The Futurists were a group of Italian artists whose credo was that "everything moves, all is in a state of flux...an outline is never stationary before our eyes, it is constantly appearing and disappearing....Given the persistence of the image on the retina, objects in movement multiply themselves incessantly...." But Futurism was more important in its ideas and aims than in its achievements, because most of the Futurist artists tried to express movement by repeating forms in slightly varying positions, as a movie camera does. They did not understand, as Villon did, that movement can be conveyed only by abstraction.

Marcel Duchamp

Villon's younger brother, Marcel Duchamp, was also interested in movement. He might be called a Cubist-Futurist. Although he was never a member of their group, his *Nude Descending a Staircase, No. 3* (Plate 56) expresses their ideas very well.

As Delaunay's *Eiffel Tower* had been the focus of criticism in Paris in 1911, Duchamp's *Nude Descending a Staircase, No. 2* was the center of controversy at the great Armory Show in New York in 1913. Americans were, at that time, far less prepared for the shattering blow of Cubism than the French had been. In New York the Armory Show became front-page news. People were shocked, scandalized, outraged, revolted, horrified, and tremendously exhilarated by the whole thing. They flocked to the show by the thousands, and their particular target was Duchamp's painting, which some wag had nicknamed "an explosion in a shingle factory."

Today Cubism has lost its "shock value." But the words Picasso used in its defense thirty years ago still apply: "The fact that for a long time Cubism has not been understood and that even today there are people who cannot see anything in it means nothing. I do not read English, an English book is a blank book to me. This does not mean that the English language does not exist. Why should I blame anyone but myself if I cannot understand what I know nothing about?"

Of course this leaves a wide opening for disagreement. One might say in reply, "And if you learn English, Mr. Picasso, so that an English book is no longer a blank book to you, that does not necessarily mean that you will enjoy what you read, or agree with it. You may, or you may not."

To which, as he is a highly intelligent man, Picasso would certainly agree.

PLATES

The Birth of Cubism

PLATE 1 PABLO PICASSO *Les Demoiselles d'Avignon,* 1907 (244 x 233 cm) New York, Museum of Modern Art (Acquired through the Lillie P. Bliss Bequest)

PLATE 2 PABLO PICASSO *Woman with a Fan*, 1908 (152 x 101 cm) Leningrad, Hermitage Museum

PLATE 3 PABLO PICASSO *Dryad*, 1908 (186 x 107 cm) Leningrad, Hermitage Museum

PLATE 4 GEORGES BRAQUE *Houses at L'Estaque*, 1908 (73 x 59.5 cm) Bern, Kunstmuseum, Herman and Margrit Rupf Foundation

PLATE 5 RAOUL DUFY *Factory at L'Estaque,* 1908 (73 x 60 cm) Beaulieu-sur-Mer, France, Henri Gaffié Collection

PLATE 6 PABLO PICASSO *Bread and Fruit Dish on a Table*, 1908 (164 x 132.5 cm) Basel, Kunstmuseum

PLATE 7 ANDRÉ DERAIN *Martigues*, 1908 (73 x 91 cm) Zürich, Kunsthaus

PLATE 8   RAOUL DUFY *Landscape at L'Estaque*, 1908 (73 x 60 cm) Beaulieu-sur-Mer, France, Henri Gaffié Collection

PLATE 9 GEORGES BRAQUE *Still Life with Fruit Bowl,* 1908–09 (52.5 x 64 cm) Stockholm, Moderna Museet

PLATE 10   PABLO PICASSO *Woman with Mandolin*, 1909 (92 x 73 cm) Leningrad, Hermitage Museum

PLATE 11 PABLO PICASSO *Fruit Bowl,* 1908 (21 x 27 cm) Basel, Kunstmuseum

PLATE 12   ANDRÉ DERAIN *Still Life on a Table*, 1910 (92 x 71 cm) Paris, Musée d'Art Moderne de la Ville de Paris

PLATE 13 PABLO PICASSO *Compote with Pears,* 1909 (92 x 73 cm) Leningrad, Hermitage Museum

PLATE 14   PABLO PICASSO *Factory at Horta de Ebro,* 1909 (53 x 60 cm) Leningrad, Hermitage Museum

PLATE 15   GEORGES BRAQUE *Guitar and Compote*, 1909 (55 x 38 cm) Bern, Kunstmuseum, Hermann and Margrit Rupf
    Foundation

Picasso, Braque, Gris

PLATE 16   PABLO PICASSO *Seated Woman*, 1909 (92 x 73 cm) London, Tate Gallery

PLATE 17   GEORGES BRAQUE *Violin and Palette,* 1910 (92 x 43 cm) New York, Solomon R. Guggenheim Museum

PLATE 18   PABLO PICASSO *Portrait of Ambroise Vollard*, 1909–10 (92 x 65 cm) Moscow, Pushkin Museum of Fine Arts

PLATE 19   PABLO PICASSO *Accordionist,* 1911 (128 x 88 cm) New York, Solomon R. Guggenheim Museum

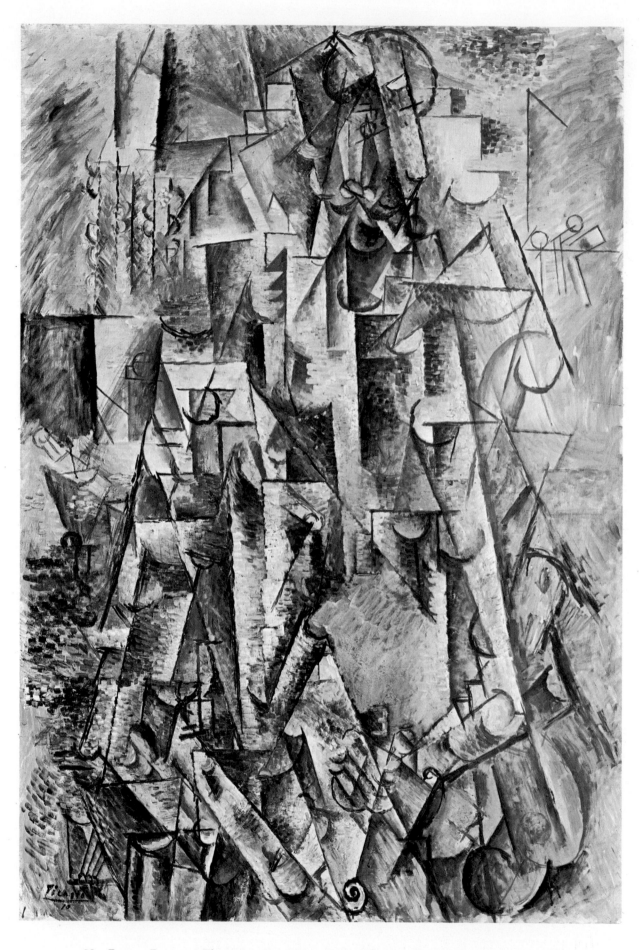

PLATE 20   PABLO PICASSO *The Poet*, 1911 (130 x 89 cm) Venice, Peggy Guggenheim Collection

PLATE 21   GEORGES BRAQUE *Still Life (Valse)*, 1912 (91.5 x 65 cm) Venice, Peggy Guggenheim Collection

PLATE 22   JUAN GRIS *Portrait of Picasso,* 1912 (92.5 x 73.8 cm) Chicago, Art Institute of Chicago (Gift of Leigh B. Block)

PLATE 23   JUAN GRIS *Gray Still Life,* 1912 (35 x 25.5 cm) Otterlo, The Netherlands, Rijksmuseum Kröller-Müller

PLATE 24   JUAN GRIS *Still Life with Oil Lamp*, 1912 (48 x 33 cm) Otterlo, The Netherlands, Rijksmuseum Kröller-Müller

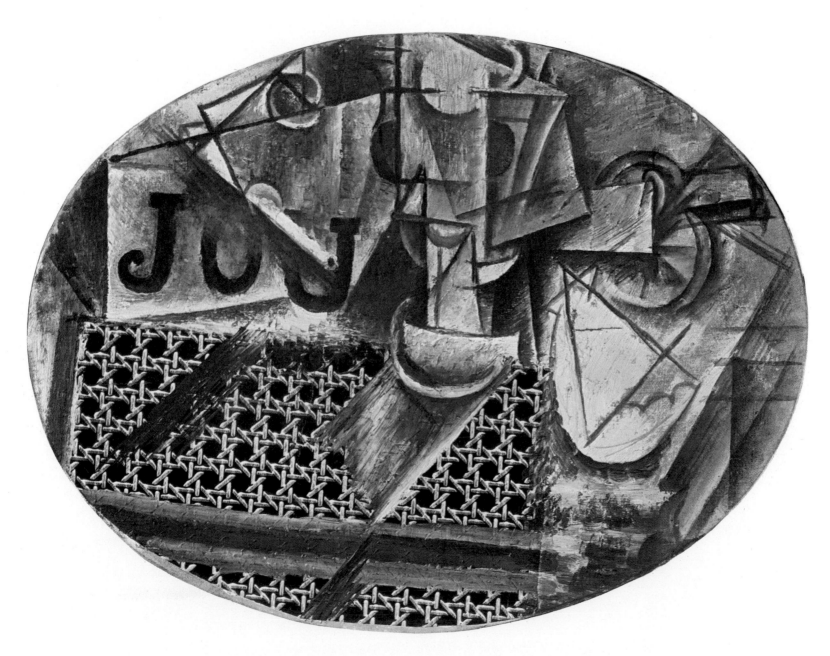

PLATE 25   PABLO PICASSO *Still Life with Chair Caning,* 1912 (29 x 37 cm) Collection of the artist

PLATE 26   GEORGES BRAQUE *Still Life on a Table*, 1912 (59.5 x 73 cm) Lucerne, Rosengart Galerie

PLATE 27 PABLO PICASSO *The Aficionado (Le Torero)*, 1912 (135 x 82 cm) Basel, Kunstmuseum

PLATE 28   PABLO PICASSO *The Violin (Jolie Eva)*, 1912 (81 x 60 cm) Stuttgart, Staatsgalerie

PLATE 29   GEORGES BRAQUE *Glass and Newspaper*, 1913 (36 x 53 cm) Zürich, private collection

PLATE 30   GEORGES BRAQUE *The Musician's Table*, 1913 (65 x 92 cm) Basel, Kunstmuseum

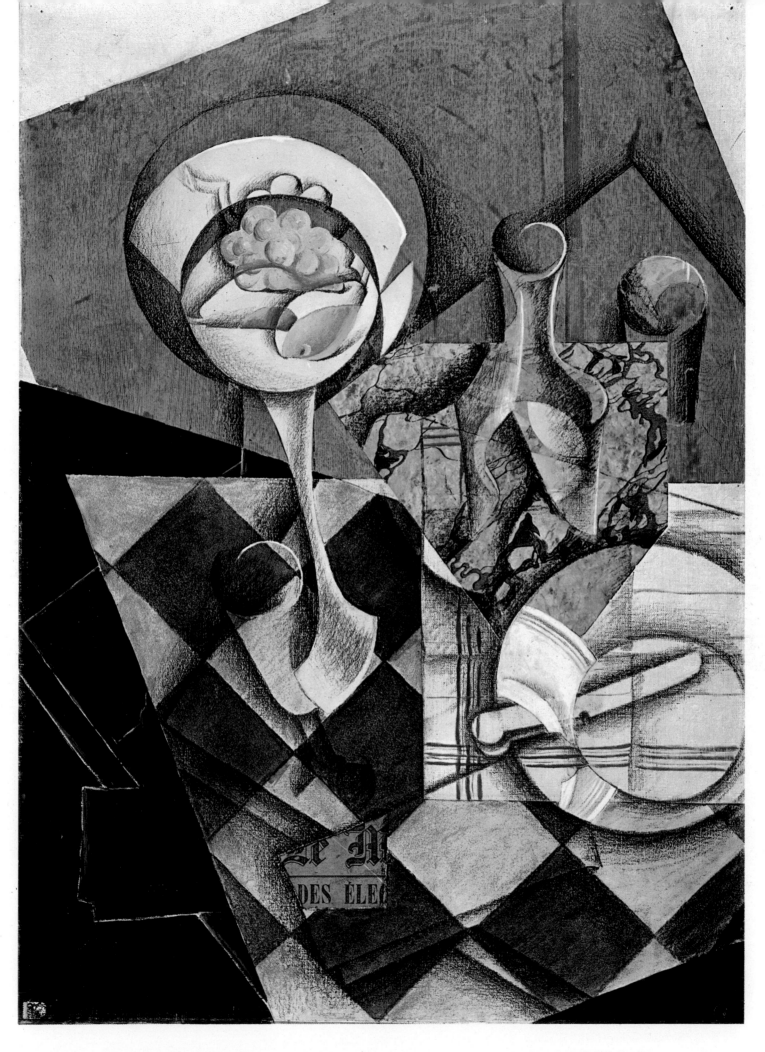

PLATE 31   JUAN GRIS *Still Life with Fruit Dish and Carafe,* 1914 (92 x 65 cm) Otterlo, The Netherlands, Rijksmuseum
Kröller-Müller

PLATE 32　Pablo Picasso *Guitar, Glass, and Fruit Bowl*, 1924 (97 x 130 cm) Zürich, Kunsthaus

PLATE 33   JUAN GRIS *Three Cards,* 1913 (65.5 x 46 cm) Bern, Kunstmuseum, Hermann and Margrit Rupf Foundation

PLATE 34 GEORGES BRAQUE *Still Life: The Table*, 1928 (80 x 129 cm) Washington, D.C., National Gallery of Art, Chester Dale Collection

PLATE 35   GEORGES BRAQUE *Still Life: Le Jour*, 1929 (113 x 144 cm) Washington, D.C., National Gallery of Art, Chester Dale Collection

PLATE 36 JUAN GRIS *House in a Landscape (Beaulieu),* 1918 (90 x 64 cm) Otterlo, The Netherlands, Rijksmuseum Kröller-Müller

Leger and Other Cubists

PLATE 37   FERNAND LÉGER *Nude Figures in a Wood*, 1909–11 (120 x 170 cm) Otterlo, The Netherlands, Rijksmuseum Kröller-Müller

PLATE 38   FERNAND LÉGER *Woman in Blue*, 1912 (194 x 130 cm) Basel, Kunstmuseum

PLATE 39   ROGER DE LA FRESNAYE *The Rower*, 1914 (60 x 80 cm) Saint-Tropez, France, Musée de l'Annonciade

PLATE 40   FERNAND LÉGER *Woman in Red and Green*, 1914 (100 x 81 cm) Paris, Musée National d'Art Moderne

PLATE 41   ROGER DE LA FRESNAYE *Factory at La Ferté-sous-Jouarre,* c. 1911 (58 x 71 cm) Paris, Musée des Arts Decoratifs (Gift of André Vera)

PLATE 42   JACQUES VILLON *Soldiers on the March,* 1913 (65 x 92 cm) Paris, Galerie Louis Carré

PLATE 43   FERNAND LÉGER *Soldier with Pipe*, 1916 (127 x 69 cm) Japan, Tokutaro Yamamura Collection

PLATE 44   ANDRÉ LHOTE *Trees*, 1914 (61 x 38 cm) Le Havre, France, Musée des Beaux-Arts

PLATE 45   Louis Marcoussis *Still Life with Checkerboard,* 1912 (139 x 93 cm) Paris, Musée National d'Art Moderne

PLATE 46　Albert Gleizes *Women Sewing*, 1913 (186 x 126 cm) Otterlo, The Netherlands, Rijksmuseum Kröller-Müller

PLATE 47   JEAN METZINGER *Woman with Fan*, 1913 (90.5 x 64 cm) New York, Solomon R. Guggenheim
Museum

PLATE 48   HENRI LE FAUCONNIER *Landscape at Meulan-Hardricourt*, 1912 (55 x 46 cm) The Hague,
Gemeentemuseum

PLATE 49   ANDRÉ LHOTE *Suburbs,* c. 1911 (48 x 38 cm) Libourne, France, Jean-Pierre Moneix Collection

PLATE 50   JEAN METZINGER *Woman with Mandolin* (100 x 73 cm) Grenoble, Musée de Peinture et de
Sculpture

PLATE 51   AUGUSTE HERBIN *View of a Village on a Hillside,* 1911 (81 x 65 cm) Otterlo, The Netherlands,
Rijksmuseum Kröller-Müller

PLATE 52   JACQUES VILLON *Portrait of Raymond Duchamp-Villon,* 1911 (36 x 27 cm) Paris, Musée National d'Art Moderne

PLATE 53   FRANK KUPKA *Plans par Couleurs*, 1910–11 (110 x 100 cm) Paris, Musée National d'Art Moderne

PLATE 54 ROBERT DELAUNAY *The Eiffel Tower*, 1910–11 (96.5 x 70.5 cm) Philadelphia, Museum of Art, Louise and Walter Arensberg Collection

PLATE 55   ROBERT DELAUNAY *The City, No. 2,* 1910 (146 x 114 cm) Paris, Musée National d'Art Moderne

PLATE 56   MARCEL DUCHAMP *Nude Descending a Staircase, No. 3*, 1916 (147.5 x 89 cm) Philadelphia,
Museum of Art, Louise and Walter Arensberg Collection

PLATE 57   MARCEL DUCHAMP *Le Passage de la Vierge à la Mariée*, 1912 (59.4 x 54 cm) New York, Museum of Modern Art

PLATE 58   FRANCIS PICABIA *Chanson Nègre*, c. 1913 (66 x 55.9 cm) New York, Metropolitan Museum of Art, Alfred Stieglitz Collection

PLATE 59   FRANCIS PICABIA *Udnie (Star Dancer on a Transatlantic Liner)*, 1913 (300 x 300 cm) Paris, Musée National d'Art Moderne

PLATE 60   FRANCIS PICABIA *Catch as Catch Can,* 1913 (98 x 80.5 cm) Philadelphia, Museum of Art, Louise and Walter Arensberg Collection

THE ARTISTS

GEORGES BRAQUE

Born at Argenteuil, May 13, 1882. In 1890 he moved with his family to Le Havre. At fifteen he began to attend classes at the School of Fine Arts with his friends Dufy and Friesz. In 1899 he gave up his studies to work with the painter-decorator Roney. In the autumn of 1900 he went to Paris to study further, and at the same time took evening courses in drawing. After a year of military service he returned to Paris in 1902. He studied at Humbert Academy, where he met Marie Laurencin and Francis Picabia, and assiduously visited the Louvre and the Luxembourg Museum, where the works of the Impressionists were collected. The following year he returned to Humbert Academy after an interval of two months at Bonnat's studio in the School of Fine Arts. In 1904 he rented a studio in Rue d'Orsel and began to paint on his own. Strongly impressed by the Fauve paintings exhibited at the Salon d'Automne in 1905, he was drawn to Fauvism, whose representatives, Matisse, Derain, and Vlaminck, he would meet in 1907. In that year he also met Picasso. The young dealer Kahnweiler, with whom he had signed a contract, introduced him to Apollinaire, and the latter went with him to the "floating laundry" studio of Picasso. In the spring and summer of 1908 he was at l'Estaque, where he had already spent the two preceding summers and where he would return in 1910. The paintings that he made there under the inspiration of Cézanne's work were rejected by the jury of the Salon d'Automne of 1908 and were exhibited in November at a one-man show organized by Kahnweiler. Regarding this show, the critic Vauxcelles, who had originated the term "Fauve" a few years earlier, was the first to speak of forms that reduce everything to "cubes." The following year Braque's friendship with Picasso was strengthened. From their discussions and experiments came Analytical Cubism.

In 1911 he introduced lettering into his painting, and in 1912 paper, sand, imitation wood, and marble appear in his pictures. At this point he had entered Cubism's Synthetic phase. Braque spent these summers with Picasso at Céret and Sorgues. At the outbreak of war in 1914 he was called to the army.

At the beginning of 1917 he was back in Paris. He began painting again and made the acquaintance of Gris and Henri Laurens. His new dealer, Leonce Rosenberg, organized a show for him in 1919; the next year he renewed his contract with Kahnweiler, and in 1928 he again exhibited in Rosenberg's gallery.

At this time his life was uneventful, and the only important dates are those of exhibitions or the beginnings of his series of works on the same subject, such as the Canefore (Basket Bearers), Mantelpieces, Tables, Marines, Billiard Tables, and Studios.

Photograph of Georges Braque

In the second forty years of his life Braque exhibited continuously at home and abroad. In Paris a room was reserved for him at the Salon d'Automne of 1942 and 1943, and in 1947 he exhibited for the first time at Maeght's gallery. Successive exhibits and retrospective shows of his work took place in Europe (Basel, 1933 and 1960; London 1934, 1946, and 1956; Brussels, 1936 and 1945; Amsterdam, 1945; Berne, 1953; Zürich, 1953; Edinburgh, 1956; Venice, 1948 and 1958; Rome, 1958). In the United States he was awarded first prize at the Carnegie International at Pittsburgh in 1937, and in 1939-40 important shows of his works were held in Chicago, Washington, and San

BRAQUE *Aria de Bach,* 1914 (63 x 50 cm) Paris, private collection

Francisco, and in 1948-49 at Cleveland and New York. In 1952 a Japanese newspaper organized an exhibit in Tokyo. During this time (1952-53) he decorated the ceiling of the Henry II room in the Louvre. Beside his main occupation as a painter, Braque designed sets for the stage, illustrated the *Theogony* of Hesiod, and worked in sculpture. In 1953-54 he designed the windows for a little church in Varengeville. In 1960 a retrospective show of his graphic work was held at the National Museum in Paris, and the following year another retrospective, "Braque's Atelier," was held at the Louvre. He died in Paris in 1963.

ROBERT DELAUNAY

Born in Paris in 1885. At the age of twenty he decided to dedicate himself to painting. At first he adopted Neo-Impressionist techniques, but later the work of Cézanne and Cubism influenced his art in decisive ways. He developed a very personal style in abstract compositions based on contrasting colors, a style which Apollinaire christened "Orphism." After 1930 he turned more definitely toward abstraction. He died at Montpellier in 1941.

ANDRÉ DERAIN

Born June 10, 1880, at Chatou, of a middle-class

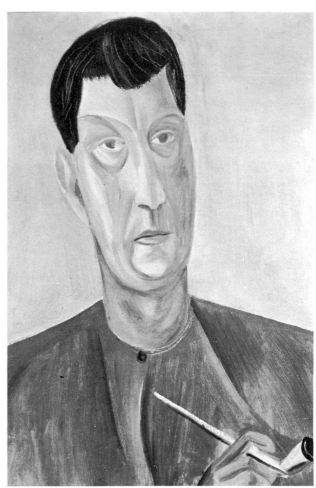

DERAIN *Self-Portrait*, 1914 (54.6 x 35.6 cm) London, from the collection of Mr. and Mrs. Eric Estorick

family. At fifteen he took his first drawing lessons from the painter Jacomin, a friend of Cézanne. Later he decided to devote himself to painting, and in 1898-99 he attended the Academy of Carriere, where he met Matisse. He became acquainted with the works of the Impressionists, of Cézanne and Gauguin, and of the old masters in the Louvre. His meeting with Vlaminck in 1900 proved decisive for the future course of his art. While doing his military service in 1903-04 he illustrated two novels by Vlaminck. Upon his return to Paris he attended the Julian Academy; the summer of 1905 he spent at Collioure with Matisse, with whom he exhibited at the Autumn Show in the famous room of the Fauves. That same year he went to London to paint; he returned to Great Britain the following year. His first meeting with Picasso was in 1906; two years later Derain, having finished his Fauve interlude, became part of the group of Montmartre painters: Picasso, Braque, Van Dongen, and Vlaminck. In 1910 he was in Spain with Picasso. Although he was close to Cubism he never accepted it completely. During these years the influence of Cézanne became enriched with various other influences: Sienese primitives,

DELAUNAY *Self-Portrait with Japanese Print*, 1905 (73 x 48.5 cm) Paris, from the collection of Mme Sonia Delaunay

Byzantine, and Gothic, which found expression in his painting of 1913-14. After doing combat duty in the World War I he turned to a more decided realism in his painting, influenced by the Renaissance, Caravaggio, the Baroque, Corot, Courbet, Delacroix, and Renoir. After a trip to Italy in 1921 he returned to France and devoted himself to portraiture with great success. He continued to paint steadily, in a representational style: landscapes, figures, allegorical and mythological scenes.

In 1935 he moved to the country, to Chambourcy. He died September 18, 1954, in Paris.

MARCEL DUCHAMP

Brother of Jacques Villon and of Raymond Duchamp-Villon, he was born at Blainville, near Rouen, in 1887. In Paris he worked at first as a librarian and attended the Julian Academy. After he joined the Cubist movement he received international fame with a painting in which he attempted to represent movement, making use of Cubist fragmentation and inspired by the "chronophotographic" analyses of Marey, which preceded motion pictures. This painting, entitled *Nude Descending a Staircase,* was exhibited in New York in 1913.

Original with Duchamp are his compositions called "ready-mades," consisting of objects in common use to which the artist has added something unusual. In 1947 he took part in the show of Surrealist painters at the Maeght Gallery in Paris.

RAOUL DUFY

Born 1877 at Le Havre. At an early age he worked as a shop clerk and took evening art courses with his friend Othon Friesz. After doing his military service he obtained a scholarship and attended, again with Friesz, the courses of Leon Bonnat at the National School of Fine Arts in Paris. He exhibited at the Show of French Artists (1901), at the Show of Independents (1903), and at the Salon d'Automne (1906), and in 1906 had his first one-man show at the Berthe Weill Gallery.

He met the Fauve painters and was especially influenced by Matisse. At this time he began to make designs for fabrics, at first for Paul Poiret and later for a factory in Lyons.

After the war of 1914-18, in which he served, his visits to Provence, Sicily, and Morocco, in 1920, 1922, and 1926 respectively, had a decided influence on his paintings of those years, which were characterized by a broad luminosity and brilliant color.

His activity was many-sided: beside his work in oils, his watercolors, and fabric designing, he also worked in ceramics, designed the set for the ballet *Palm Beach,* and illustrated many books. In 1937 he made an immense panel, sixty by ten meters, which he exhibited at the World's Fair in Paris. In his last years he had exhibits in Paris (1948), New York (1951), Geneva (1952) and received an award at the Venice Biennial of 1952.

He died at Forcalquier in Provence in 1953.

ALBERT GLEIZES

Born 1881 in Paris. During his youth he came under the influence of Impressionism, but after 1906 he turned to greater simplification of color and was drawn to Cubism. He was one of the group called the "Section d'Or," which often met at his home or at Jacques Villon's studio in Puteaux.

He was the author, with Metzinger, of the treatise *On Cubism* published in 1912.

During World War I he was in America, and there underwent a spiritual crisis that led him to a deep piety. From that time on his work was imbued with religious feeling. He died at seventy-two in Avignon in 1953.

JUAN GRIS

José Victoriano Gonzales, who later took the name

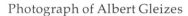

Photograph of Albert Gleizes

Juan Gris, was born in Madrid on March 23, 1887. As a very young man he worked as illustrator for the reviews *Blanco y Negro* and *Madrid Comico*, and in 1904, after having studied at the School of Arts and Trades at Madrid, he enrolled in a painting class at the studio of José Maria Carbonero. In 1906 he went to Paris and soon became part of the intimate group of artists and intellectuals who gathered at Picasso's studio. In the meantime he worked for several magazines *L'Assiette au Beurre*, *Le Charivari, Le Temoin* and in 1908 became acquainted with the dealer Kahnweiler, with whom he signed a contract several years later.

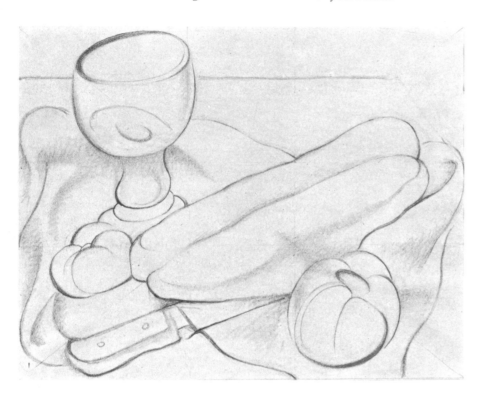

Gris *Bread*, 1920 (25.7 x 33.5 cm) Paris, Galerie Louise Leiris

His first Cubist painting was done in 1911. The following year he took part in the Show of Independents, exhibiting a portrait of Picasso, and also showed with the Section d'Or. At this time he met Josette, the woman who was to be with him for the rest of his life. In 1913 he spent the summer working with Picasso at Céret, in the eastern Pyrenees, and during the following winter he devoted himself to experiments with *papiers colles*.

During World War I, since Kahnweiler had had to take refuge in Switzerland, Gris found himself in ever-increasing financial difficulties. In 1916 he solved his difficulties by selling his entire output to the dealer Leonce Rosenberg, and so was able to spend the rest of the war years in Touraine. In 1919 he had his first large one-man show at "L'Effort Moderne" of Rosenberg. In 1922 he made his home at Boulogne-sur-Seine. He exhibited in

Paris and abroad, worked at etching and lithography, but his health was poor. He died at Boulogne-sur-Seine on May 11, 1927.

AUGUSTE HERBIN

Born at Quévy, April 29, 1882. After becoming acquainted with Cubism he exhibited in 1910 at the Show of Independents, in the same room with Albert Gleizes, Jean Metzinger, and Fernand Léger. After 1912 Herbin turned toward abstract art, and in 1932 founded the group called "Abstraction-Creation." He died in January of 1960.

FRANK KUPKA

Born at Opocno (Bohemia) in 1878, he fled his home after his father's second marriage. He was taken in by Professor Studnicka, who interested him in the study of art. He studied at the Academy of Fine Arts in Prague and later in that of Vienna. In 1894 he settled in Paris, earning his living as a cartoonist. He came under the influence of the Fauves and later of Cubism. Then after 1911 he turned to abstraction. He died at Puteaux in 1957.

ROGER DE LA FRESNAYE

Born in 1885 at Le Mans. He completed his secondary studies with a brilliant record, his interest at the time being in science. In 1903 he enrolled at the Julian Academy, then at the School of Fine Arts, and in 1908 at Ranson Academy, where the instruction of Denis and Serusier had a decisive influence on his artistic future. About 1912 he

Kupka *Self-Portrait with Pipe*, 1910 (46 x 55 cm) Prague, Narodni Galerie

adopted Cubism, but was drafted at the outbreak of World War I, which put an end to his development along Cubist lines. After the war he turned to traditional painting, seeking the purity of drawing of the Florentines. He died at Grasse in 1925.

LÉGER *The Smoker*, 1914, Paris, Frigerio Collection

HENRI LE FAUCONNIER

Born at Hesdin, near Calais, in July 1881. About 1910 he turned to art as a career, coming under the influence of Cubism. A solid and austere painter, he was a friend of writers of the Abbaye group, among them Jules Romain and Georges Duhamel. He left France for a long stay in Holland, where he was regarded as head of the movement. He died in Paris in January of 1946.

FERNAND LÉGER

Born February 4, 1881, at Argentan in Normandy. From 1890 to 1896 he studied at the Argentan College and at the religious school of Tinchebray. Later he worked in architectural studios in Caen and, after 1900, in Paris. After his military service he enrolled in 1903 at the School of Decorative Arts in Paris, and took courses at several private schools. In 1906, after a severe illness and a long period of convalescence in Corsica, he returned to Paris and devoted himself entirely to painting. Although he was influenced by the work of Cézanne, Henri Rousseau, and by Cubism, he developed a very personal artistic style.

He was a friend of Villon, Delauney, Gleizes, Picabia, and Kupka, with whom he formed the group of the Section d'Or. He fought in World War I and in 1920 began his collaboration with the architect Le Corbusier. He was very active: in addition to executing murals he taught a course in painting, gave lectures, and in 1924 made a film called *Mechanical Ballet*. During World War II he lived in the United States, where he taught at Yale University and other places. In 1945 he returned to France, took part in political demonstrations, traveled, and worked at architectural decoration. In 1949, the year of a large exhibit of his work at the Museum of Modern Art in Paris, he devoted himself to ceramics at Biot. Another show of his work was held at the Tate Gallery in London in 1950. Among the works carried out in the succeeding years are the large mural panel for the United Nations building in New York and windows for various churches. The last year of his life, 1955, was intensely busy. He received first prize at the San Paolo Biennial, a large retrospective show of his work was held at Lyons, and he made murals for the plants of Gaz de France. After returning from a trip to Prague he died at his home in Gif-sur-Yvette on August 17.

LÉGER *Composition*, 1917, Milan, private collection of modern art

ANDRÉ LHOTE

Born July 5, 1885, at Bordeaux. For ten years he worked with a sculptor in his home city. Self-taught, he learned to appreciate the work of the Impressionists, of Gauguin, and, later in Paris, of Cézanne. He began early to exhibit at the Salon d'Automne and the Salon des Independents. He was included in the first Cubist shows and later belonged to the group Section d'Or.

From 1918 he taught in various schools; he founded his own in 1922. In addition to being active as a teacher, by means of which he exercised a considerable influence, he was also a critic and theoretician and the author of the *Treatise on Landscape* and *Treatise on the Figure*. He died in Paris in 1962.

LOUIS MARCOUSSIS

Louis Markous, who changed his surname to Marcoussis, was born in Warsaw in 1878. In 1903 he settled in Paris; he attended the classes of Jules Lefebvre and painted in the Impressionist manner until 1907. Then he adopted Cubism and became part of the group of artists of the Section d'Or who gathered around Jacques Villon. After the war his style, although still Cubist, showed a greater tendency toward realism.

Metzinger *Portrait of Guillaume Apollinaire,* 1910 (57 x 48 cm) Paris, Musée National d'Art Moderne

He died, at sixty-three, in Cusset (Allier) in 1941.

JEAN METZINGER

Born at Nantes in 1883. He soon revealed his ar-

Metzinger *Portrait of Albert Gleizes,* 1911, Paris, Musée National d'Art Moderne (Photo: Giraudon)

tistic talent, beginning to paint while still very young. On his arrival in Paris he refused traditional art instruction, adhering first to Neo-Impressionism and then to Fauvism. In 1908 he joined the Cubists, with whom he remained for the rest of his career.

He was one of the group of painters of the Section d'Or. With Albert Gleizes he was the author of the treatise *On Cubism* published in Paris in 1912.

He died in Paris in 1956.

FRANCIS PICABIA

Born January 22, 1878, in Paris, of a Spanish father and French mother. His artistic gifts were apparent very early. He studied with Cormon at the School of Fine Arts and at the School of Decorative Arts. His early paintings are in an Impressionist style; in 1908 he adopted Cubism. In 1912 and 1913 he painted his most important works and took part in the Sunday meetings of the group of the Section d'Or in Jacques Villon's studio at

Puteaux. In 1915 he was in New York, where he met Duchamp and began the newspaper *391*, which was the beginning of the Dada movement. In 1924 he made the sets for the ballet *Relâche* for Rolf de Mare and the film *Entr'acte*. His great

Photograph of Francis Picabia

versatility led him to surprising stylistic changes: after passing through a representational phase, he turned in 1945 to abstract art. He died in Paris in 1953.

PABLO PICASSO

Born at Malaga in Spain on October 25, 1881. He was early attracted to the profession of his father, who was a teacher of drawing. In 1891, the year in which his family moved to La Coruña, he began to attend the School of Fine Arts and to paint, revealing an exceptional talent. In 1895 the family moved to Barcelona, where he continued his studies at the local art school. Later he went to Madrid for various academic studies. In 1897, already possessed of great technical ability, he was attracted to the artistic avant-garde of Barcelona, which was imbued with humanism and symbolism. Among the poets, writers, and artists with whom he became acquainted were Baroja, Manolo, d'Ors, Sabartes, Nonell, Casas, Sunyer, Soler, and Casagamas. This atmosphere profoundly influenced him and aroused in him

the desire to go where this movement was most intensely alive, to Paris.

His first trip to the artistic capital of Europe was in September of 1900, and his stay, except for a brief return to Spain to launch, with Soler, the review *Arte Joven,* lasted until the end of 1901. Although most of his friends were Spanish artists, among them Iturrino, Gargallo, and Gonzales, he also became acquainted with Coquiot and Max Jacob. Through the latter he held, with Iturrino, an exhibit at Vollard's gallery.

Until the spring of 1904 he moved back and forth between Barcelona and Paris, where his circle of friends and interests was expanding. In 1904 he settled definitely in Paris, in the famous *bateau-lavoir* of Place Ravignan. In the course of a few years his studio became a meeting place for such personalities as Jacob, Jarry, Raynal, Salmon, Reverdy, Apollinaire, and the Steins. In this peaceful but economically straitened atmosphere he passed from his Blue period to the more formal, classical harmonies of his Rose period.

In 1905 he met Fernande Olivier. With her, during the summer of 1906, he went to Barcelona, Gosol, and Lerida, and was deeply impressed by Romanesque sculpture and by pre-Roman Iberian sculpture. At this same time he met Matisse, the head of the new Fauve movement, and, perhaps through his influence, became enthusiastic over primitive African sculpture. During the winter of 1906-07 he began sketches for *Les Demoiselles d'Avignon*, on which he worked a long time but

PICASSO *Still Life*, 1910 (64.3 x 49.1 cm) collection of the artist

which he left unfinished after many re-workings. He signed a contract with Kahnweiler by means of which he could live more comfortably, and became acquainted with Braque and Derain: the former was still experimenting in a Fauve style, and the latter was involved with structural problems related to Cézanne, which he was resolving in a pre-Cubist style.

In the summer of 1909 he painted Cubist landscapes at Horta de San Juan; these were exhibited that autumn by Vollard, and he had a show at the Thannhauser Gallery in Monaco. Although he did not exhibit at the Salons, his paintings were avidly studied by the most advanced of the young artists, and his work was the heart of the Cubist movement. In 1910 he spent the summer working at Cadaques with Derain, the following summer with Braque at Ceret, returning each time to Paris with a prodigious quantity of richly inventive paintings.

By now in the wake of the Spanish painter there was a whole squadron of young artists, not all of whom were able to understand the realistic complexity of his structural language. In addition to Léger and Gris, who were certainly the best,

PICASSO *Landscape*, 1908 (64 x 49.5 cm) Bern, Kunstmuseum, Hermann and Margrit Rupf Collection

PICASSO *Head*, 1909 (63.5 x 47 cm) Paris, private collection

there were many followers, from Gleizes to Metzinger, from Herbin to Marcoussis, Delaunay to Roger de La Fresnaye, from the Italian Futurists to Villon, Duchamp, and Picabia, to mention the most noted. After his break with Fernande

Olivier, he fell in love with Marcelle Humbert (Eva), whose name appears in many pictures.

His fame continually increased in France and abroad, partly due to Kahnweiler, who wrote a very intelligent history of Cubism. At the international exhibits in Monaco, Cologne, and Berlin, Picasso's Cubist paintings stood out strongly. In the international avant-garde reviews his works were published, and in the most advanced artistic circles his innovations were discussed. The name Picasso became the banner of modernity.

At the outbreak of World War I in 1914 Picasso stayed in Paris. He was saddened by the death of Eva in the winter of 1915-16. In the spring of 1917 he made a trip to Italy, where he met the dancer Olga Koklova, whom he married the following year. He came under the influence of classical art and the carefree gaiety of the *commedia dell'arte*, and in collaboration with Diaghilev, director of the Ballet Russe, and the modern composers Stravinsky and Satie, he found a creative stimulus which manifested itself in a number of stage sets that gave new life to this branch of art.

In the following years Picasso's activity followed two distinct bents, classical and Cubist. He also became acquainted with several experimental

poets, among them Breton and Eluard, who were to initiate Surrealism. In 1925 he took part in the first Surrealist show in Paris. The same year saw the beginning of his Neo-Romantic period, signaled by the *Three Dancers*. In 1932 at Boisgeloup he returned with greater facility to the sculpture he had begun the year before, profiting by his technical collaboration with Julio Gonzales, especially in metal sculpture. At this time he met Marie Therese Walter, by whom he had a child, Maia, in 1935—fourteen years earlier Koklova had given him a son, Paul. In the preceding years Picasso had returned to illustration, which he had never completely abandoned after 1911: he illustrated works of Ovid, Balzac, Aristophanes, Buffon, and Gongora. He was also very active in the field of engraving.

At the outbreak of the Spanish Civil War, Picasso was on the side of the Republicans, and accepted the position of director of the Prado, carrying out the important work of saving from destruction the immense artistic patrimony of Spain. The horrors of war and blind human bestiality left a dramatic imprint on his work up to 1945. During this period, in which his companion was Dora Maar, he lived mainly in Paris, where he met Sartre and Giacometti. In 1941 he wrote a dramatic script, worked at sculpture, and painted furiously.

Immediately after the war, from 1946 to 1948, he lived at Antibes, where his insatiable desire to experiment with new materials led him to terra cotta and ceramics, with extraordinarily happy results. This was a time of rediscovered tranquility, when Françoise Gilot, his next companion, gave him two sons, Claude and Paloma. After 1948 he lived at Vallauris for six years. Here it was lithography that attracted him, and with his prodigious versatility he succeeded in giving this technique new life. After his break with Gilot he married Jacqueline Roque. An intense period of participation in international political life, especially around 1948-50—years in which he traveled to Poland, Italy, and England—was followed by seclusion with his friendships and his work.

JACQUES VILLON

Gaston Duchamp, who took the name of Jacques Villon, was born at Damville (Eure) in 1875, twelve years before his brother Marcel, who also became a painter. After working with a notary at Rouen he settled in Paris in 1894. During his first years in Paris he earned his living as a satirical cartoonist. From about 1906 he devoted himself to painting, influenced at first by the work of Degas and Toulouse-Lautrec. In 1911 he embraced Analytical Cubism. It was around Villon that the group formed which was called the Section d'Or, including among others Léger, Gleizes, Kupka, Picabia, La Fresnaye, and Metzinger.

List of Illustrations

Printed in Italy by A. Mondadori - Verona